Step-by-Step Bond Investing

A Beginner's Guide to the Best Investments and Safety in the Bond Market

Joseph Hogue

About this Book

Of all the opportunities to invest and make money, bonds are likely one of the most neglected. Stocks are the get-rich investment, hyped by Wall Street and favored by investors. Commodities are widely used to hedge risk and to gamble on price changes. Even real estate is more widely held for its cash flow and other benefits.

According to research by fund manager Vanguard, the average investor holds just 15% of their portfolio in bonds. Since older investors typically hold much more of their investments in fixed-income, it's safe to assume that many younger investors are neglecting the investment all together.

What you might not realize is that bonds are critical to reaching your financial goals. No other investment provides the kind of safety and security you'll get from bonds and few other investments provide the kind of cash flow you'll get from these fixed-income opportunities.

In fact, manage your bonds right and you might not need much more to meet your financial goals. You'll get stable returns for decades and won't have to worry about constant crashes in stock prices. You'll get nearly guaranteed cash flows to pay for expenses and the retirement you deserve.

Putting a portfolio of bonds together that will meet your goals can be surprisingly easy if you know where to start. Understand bond basics and how to avoid the mistakes that cost other investors money and you'll find an investment that's easier to manage than any other while moving you closer to financial freedom.

This book will do exactly that, help you put together a step-by-step strategy in bonds to understand how much of your portfolio to invest and how to do it.

In this book you'll learn:

- The five risks in bond investing, which can be reduced and how to avoid some altogether (pg. 12)

- Why investors neglect bonds and how you can use the asset class to reach your goals (pg. 17)

- The four types of bonds that should be in everyone's portfolio (pg. 26)

- How to put together a simple bond investing strategy to cover monthly living expenses without having to sell your investments (pg. 41)

- How to manage your bond investing strategy to minimize costs and maximize return (pg. 57)

Check out the other three books in the Step-by-Step Investing series to round out your investing strategy. You'll get everything you need to lay out a sleep-at-night investing strategy that will meet your financial goals.

I've put nearly a decade of work as an investment analyst into the series and hope you can use it to develop a simple strategy that will meet your goals. If you find the ideas useful, please leave a review on Amazon to let others know.

Joseph Hogue, CFA

Born and raised in Iowa, Joseph Hogue graduated from Iowa State University after serving in the Marine Corps. He worked in corporate finance and real estate before starting a career in investment analysis. Mr. Hogue has appeared on Bloomberg as an expert in emerging market investing and has led a team of equity analysts for sell-side research. His investment analysis has been featured in advisor newsletters, institutional research reports and in the financial press.

He holds the Chartered Financial Analyst (CFA) designation, the gold standard for ethical and professional conduct in investment management.

PeerFinance101.com is a new kind of personal finance blog where readers share their own stories of personal finance challenges and success. There's no one-size-fits-all solution to meeting your financial goals but you'll find a lot of similarities in others' stories and a lot of ideas that will help you get through your own challenges.

Click through to PeerFinance101 for topics from investing to managing debt as well as retirement planning and frugal living.

Step-by-Step Investing: A Beginner's Guide to the Best Investments in Stocks

ISBN-13 (eBook) 978-0-9971112-0-0
ISBN-13 (Print) 978-0-9971112-1-7

Contents

Bonds: The Neglected Path to Financial Freedom

If you're reading this book, you probably know more than most people about bonds or are at least interested in the opportunity for investment.

Congratulations, you're already way ahead of the curve and on the way to a safer, more balanced investing strategy.

Whenever I switch a conversation from stocks to bonds, expressions go blank and people tune out. While stocks are almost universally understood as an investment strategy, most investors know almost nothing about bonds. Just mentioning the word brings up images of slick junk-bond traders of the 80's. Start a discussion of how bond prices move with interest rates and inflation and you might as well be speaking another language.

Most investors think investing in bonds is just too complicated or only for Wall Street traders.

The truth is that investing in bonds is likely the best investment you can make when planning your financial future. Unlike stocks, bonds provide a nearly certain return that can be planned over decades. You don't have to follow your bonds regularly like you might an investment in stocks and most of the analysis work is already done for you.

Bonds are not as complicated as you may think either. In fact, you've probably already held a bond and didn't even know it. Anytime someone has given you an IOU for a loan, you received a bond. You might not have received interest on the loan and it wasn't as legally binding as a bond, but all the basic ideas were there.

What are bonds?

If you need $10 to get you through the week, you just have to ask politely. Need $10 million to get you through the year and you'll have to do more than just say please.

While a business might be making sales and booking profits, cash doesn't always come in immediately. Land that dream contract and you may need money for supplies well before you get paid on the order. Even governments need cash to pay for programs and expenses before annual taxes start rolling in.

As a business owner, you could sell stock ownership in your company but that means sharing the profits with investors. Bank loans are one option but may not be offered on terms you need or at a rate you can afford.

Enter bonds, a loan sold to investors with a fixed payment and payoff date.

Everyone from companies to governments, local municipalities and housing authorities can take out loans secured by a bond. Since bond investments are backed by assets and a contract, investors are willing to loan the money at lower rates. Companies can also use interest paid on the loan to reduce the amount of taxes they pay on income.

Bonds are a critical part of financing for small businesses. While taking out loans includes some financial risk, it means more profits for the owners and lower costs to operate the company.

Bonds are always issued for a specific face value, sometimes called par value and usually $1,000 for each certificate. Companies plan out their cash needs for years in advance, how much in expenses can be paid through sales and how much additional cash they might need.

To raise the extra money, the company will make a bond offer including the total amount of the loan, an interest rate offered and how long until the loan will be paid off.

Most bonds pay a fixed rate of interest over the life of the loan, called its maturity. The company pays only interest over the period and then returns the face value of the bonds to investors at the maturity date.

The interest payments on bonds are usually paid twice a year and are called coupons because bonds used to have cut-out coupons that you mailed in to collect your payment. Nearly everything is handled digitally now. Your interest payments will go straight to your investment account and you might not even get a paper certificate of your bonds.

After putting together the details of the bond offer, the company then pays a credit rating agency like Standard & Poor's or Moody's to look over the offer and rate the bonds. This involves looking at the ability of the company to pay back the loan, what kind of collateral the company is putting up to cover the loan and other factors.

The rating is important because it helps investors understand the risk involved in the investment. Like all investments, the amount of risk determines the level of return investors require to take on the risk. Backed by the "full faith and credit of the United States," bonds issued by the U.S. government are said to be risk-free and so investors are willing to park their money for little more than a savings account. Bonds issued by very small companies are not nearly as safe so investors demand a higher return.

So if McDonald's needs to raise $100 million for an expansion project or other cash needs, it might issue 100,000 bonds of $1,000 each. It agrees to pay an interest rate of 4% over 30 years and then return the $100 million to investors at the end of that period. An investor holding a $1,000 bond will receive $20 every six months, $40 or 4% annually on the face value. Depending on the coupon interest rate and the rating, you might pay more or less than $1,000 for each bond but we'll get into that later in the book.

Bonds are issued for periods from a year to as long as 99 years but most companies issue shorter-term bonds for five to 30 years. The number of years to maturity is an important factor in the interest rate that investors demand for the bond.

Bonds with less than five years left to maturity are referred to as short-term bonds, while those with five to 12 years left are called intermediate bonds and those with more than 12 years left are referred to as long-term bonds.

For investors

We'll go into detail what bond investing can mean for your portfolio but generally investing in bonds means safety and stable income. Bonds are often backed by a company's assets and the payments are set by contract. Interest payments must be paid before the owners or stockholders get anything. If the company runs into trouble, bondholders have a right to the company's assets in a bankruptcy and may get some of their investment back while stockholders will likely get nothing.

Investing in different bonds lets investors customize their portfolio exactly to their needs for cash and returns. Bonds with longer maturities mean higher rates of return while bonds that get paid off sooner mean less risk and opportunities to reinvest the money. Bonds of the highest-rated companies means protection of your investment while riskier bonds can amplify your returns but still involve less risk than stocks.

Most likely, you already have money in bonds and may not even know it. Most of the $40 trillion U.S. bond market is held by life insurance companies, banks and pension funds. These big money players need to earn a return on their money that will cover their future commitments but look to the safety of the bond market for protection.

Why should every investor hold bonds?

The stock market has crashed ten times since 1929 with several episodes wiping out half of the value in investors' portfolios. While stocks eventually rebound, many investors never enjoy the benefit of long-term gains as they panic-sell at the low point only to buy back in when prices peak.

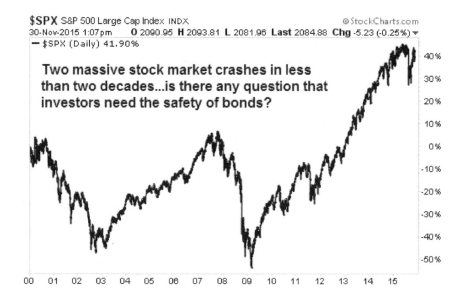

But you're a buy-and-hold investor, holding onto your stocks through good times and bad. You don't have to worry about a temporary setback in prices, right?

What happens when that setback happens just as you're about to retire? I recently interviewed one investor for a blog post that found himself exactly in that situation.

Travis was ready to retire at 63 years old after 35 years in publishing. He had saved and invested his whole life and was ready to reap the rewards and find his sandy beach somewhere. He had 70% of his retirement account in stocks and another 10% in real estate funds.

The year was 2008.

By the end of that year, Travis had lost a third of his retirement and had worried enough. He went to a financial advisor to assess his situation and reallocate his money to safer investments like bonds. If you had told him the market would rebound in a few years, he says he would have shook his head and said, "I'm just ready to be done with it. I don't want to lose anymore sleep."

Travis eventually retired at 67 in 2012 though it was on more modest goals than planned. His story isn't so uncommon and one that can easily be avoided with a bond investing strategy.

Not only do bonds provide a much more certain return when compared to stocks, but they are almost completely uncorrelated with stock prices.

That idea of correlation is an important one in investing and just means that prices do not follow each other. If one investment is uncorrelated with another, when one goes down...it won't take the other down with it.

In fact, when the stock market fell by 56% over the 17 months to March 2009, the U.S. bond market gained 7.4% over the period.

Bonds are more than just a safety play for your portfolio. For many people, bonds provide consistent cash flow to pay living expenses. Other investments yield dividends and put cash in your pocket but few do it with the certainty and consistency of bonds.

Risks in Bond Investing

The risks in bond investing are very different from those you might know from investing in the stock market. Most bond risks arise from the fact of fixed payments over the life of the investment. Some of these risks can be reduced while some can be almost completely ignored depending on how long you hold your bonds.

Interest rate risk is one of the most talked about for bonds but really isn't as much an issue for those that don't sell their bonds. Hold your bonds to maturity and you don't have to worry much about one of the biggest risks...how's that for a bond investing secret?

Everyone else has to worry about interest rate risk because bond prices fall when rates go up. The reason is pretty simple.

If you're holding a bond that pays 5% interest payments against current market rates of 4% then you're doing pretty well, right? Now if market interest rates go up to 6% the deal doesn't look so great. You can't change the interest payments on the bond, that's why they're called fixed-income investments. You still get the same amount, the face value of the bond, at maturity as well.

So if bond payments don't change when market rates change, how do investors sell their bonds if they don't want to hold them to maturity? They're going to have to lower the price to compete with the new, higher rates in the market.

It works in the other direction as well. If interest rates go down, then those existing bonds with interest rates set when the market was paying more start looking pretty good. Investors raise their prices when they sell the bonds.

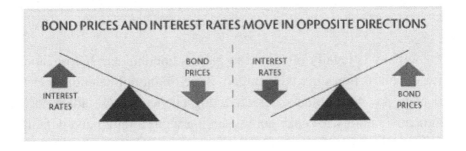

BOND PRICES AND INTEREST RATES MOVE IN OPPOSITE DIRECTIONS

Interest rate risk is greater for bonds with more years to maturity. You'd have to lower the price more to persuade an investor to buy that 5% rate bond and hold it for many years.

Again though, if you're holding your bonds to maturity, you will always get the fixed payments and the face value. You are going to get the yield-to-maturity from when you bought the bond.

Reinvestment risk is the cruel twist to interest rate risk. When rates decrease, you might be able to sell your bonds for a higher price but what are you going to do with that money? The rate at which you can reinvest that money is now lower.

While interest rate risk isn't an issue if you hold your bonds to maturity, reinvestment risk still bites. You can't do much about it and it's been socking it to investors since the early 1980s. The rate on the 10-year Treasury has dropped from nearly 15% to just above two percent over the last three decades.

It would be hard to imagine rates following the same path over the next 30 years unless the government starts charging you to hold your money. Reinvestment risk might not be as big an issue as rates increase but investors selling their bonds may start feeling the bite of interest rate risk.

Default risk is one of the worst risks for long-term investors. You won't have to worry about the U.S. government making its bond payments but everyone else is a big question mark.

A company is legally obligated to pay its bondholders before stock owners but if times get bad enough, there might not be enough cash to even pay bondholders. Credit rating agencies look closely at a company's ability to repay debt when it assigns a rating and defaults on investment grade bonds are rare.

Bonds of emerging market countries and junk-rated corporate debt default more frequently. If a company defaults, your interest payments will stop and you may not get the face value maturity payment either.

One of two things usually happens in a default. If there is absolutely no way out and no future for the company, it may be liquidated. In this case, bondholders may get pennies on the dollar for their bonds depending on how much money is left after paying higher-ranked creditors.

If the company wants to continue doing business, it may try to renegotiate with its bondholders. This will be done between an arbiter or judge and a group representing creditors. You may have to take a cut on the value of your bonds and may have to accept longer-dated bonds but you'll get more than in a liquidation.

Default risk can be minimized by holding fewer high-risk bonds and buying many individual bonds in each rating category. Diversification means that one default won't hit your returns too badly. There is a reason junk bonds pay rates of 6% against rates of 4% for investment-grade bonds. Some of the bonds in the category are going to default and your actual return is going to come down a little.

Despite the severity of default risk in bonds, it actually happens pretty infrequently for most investments. The average default rate for all corporate bonds is less than 1% with less than half a percent of the highest rated bonds defaulting in any given year.

Downgrade risk is another one that you shouldn't have to worry about too much if you hold your bonds to maturity. Credit rating agencies like Moody's assign a rating when a bond is issued but review the company regularly for its ability to pay the debt. If the company falls on tough times, the rating agency may lower the bond rating because of higher risk of default.

Downgrading a bond's rating has the same effect as higher interest rates. A riskier bond isn't as attractive to new investors. Since the coupon and maturity payment can't be changed, the price is going to have to come down to persuade new buyers.

Bond ratings can be upgraded as well but it doesn't happen as often. Traders sit around all day buying and selling bonds ahead of a possible upgrade or downgrade, trying to make a quick profit. Stay out of this game and just hold your bonds to maturity. You'll save money in fees and won't have to worry about many of the risks in bonds.

Inflation risk is another of the worst bond risks for long-term investors because it's the most uncertain. Your bonds pay a fixed payment whether inflation heads higher or not.

The current 10-year Treasury rate of 2.25% is about half a percent above the annual rate of inflation. That means the return keeps your money buying the same amount of stuff and 0.55% more each year. If inflation increases to 3% then Treasury investors are actually losing money on their bonds. Of course, an increase of inflation usually takes interest rates up with it. New bonds will offer higher rates but old bonds are going to be hit hard.

I've been surprised, along with many other analysts, how low inflation has stayed for so many years. Governments around the world are pumping out money like its on sale and yet prices in the United States, Europe and Japan continue to grow very slowly.

As with the downward trend in rates, it's equally difficult to imagine inflation staying as low as it is now. The ten-year average rate of inflation is around three percent, nearly double its current rate.

Higher inflation doesn't mean you have to lose money on your bond investments. When inflation increases, new bonds pay higher rates. By having some bonds maturing in different years, called laddering, you will be able to constantly buy more bonds at higher rates.

That's a lot of risk

The risks to bond investing, especially the fact that many are tied to economic concepts like rates and inflation, make the investment a tough sell to investors. The idea of facing these risks for low single-digit returns doesn't sound very appealing to most.

But don't forget that many of these risks will not significantly affect long-term investors that hold their bonds to maturity. Despite the risks to bond prices, the risks to bond investors are very manageable for the buy-and-hold investor.

One study of the period between 1950 and 1999 found that the stock market was three times more volatile than the bond market. Since that time, the stock prices have been more than four times as volatile as the bond market. For investors that don't want to lose sleep over their money when Wall Street claims the sky is falling, bonds are the ultimate in stability.

Trade in and out of your bonds and you'll face every one of the risks listed above and can lose a lot of money in the process. Hold your bonds to maturity and benefit from one of the most stable investments you will find.

Understanding Bond Prices and Returns

If you're going to trade your bonds, you'll need to understand how a mountain of economic data and expectations will affect prices on a minute-to-minute basis. If you are going to use bonds as a part of your long-term investing strategy, holding your bonds until they mature, you really don't need more than the basics.

Bond valuation and investing can be just as complicated as stocks – or it can be extremely easy.

There are a number of rates or yield measures that you will want to know about when investing in bonds. These all measure some kind of return available and will help determine whether you want to include a bond in your portfolio.

The first is the **coupon rate**, which is the annual amount of interest collected divided by the face value of the bond. It's the percentage amount the company decides to pay on the bonds. Historically, bond certificates included coupons that would be torn off to redeem the semi-annual payments.

If you know the coupon rate but want to find the amount of interest paid each year, just multiply the rate times the face value.

Since the coupon payments on a bond never change and you will always receive the face value of the bond at maturity, the only thing that can change on the investment is the price. This brings us to the most basic lesson in bonds, how interest rates affect prices.

Interest rates and bond prices

Interest rates are the cost of money, whether to borrow or invest. The Federal Reserve, the monetary authority of the United States, sets an interest rate for bank borrowing to influence the economy. If the economy gets going too fast and inflation rises, the Fed increases rates to make borrowing more expensive. If economic growth slows, the Fed lowers rates to make borrowing cheaper.

The rate set by the Fed flows through to all other interest rates, pushing interest rates for business borrowing, credit cards and everything else higher or lower. An interest rate isn't only the cost of a loan but also the return that the lender receives on that loan. So interest rates affect the investment returns required by investors to make an investment.

To lock their money up for longer periods of time, investors are generally going to require a greater return. To make a relatively short two-year loan, an investor might only require a percent or two return. Ask that same investor to lock their money up in a 30-year loan and they'll want a much higher return.

This tradeoff between time and interest rates is called the yield curve. It's the yield curve on U.S. Treasury bonds that help determine the amount of interest received and bond pricing on other bonds.

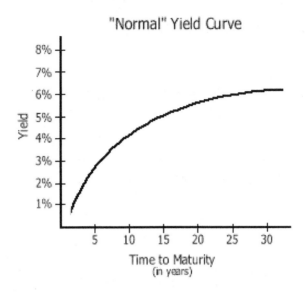

"Normal" Yield Curve

Yield (vertical axis) vs. *Time to Maturity (in years)* (horizontal axis)

How do interest rates and the yield curve affect bond prices? If interest rates increase, shifting the yield curve higher, then investors will make more money on their new investments.

That bond you bought before rates increased still pays the same amount and will yield you the same return on the price you paid. That return might not be so attractive to new investors since they can make more money on other investments after the increase in rates.

To make the return on an older bond competitive with other investments, the price must change to attract investors. Imagine you paid $950 for a bond that paid $47.50 a year in coupon payments for a 5% yield. That 5% yield might have been great until interest rates increase and other investments are paying 5.5% annually. Nobody is going to buy that bond yielding 5% if they can get a new bond and make 5.5% a year.

Since the $47.50 coupon payment doesn't change, you might need to lower the price to $863 which would increase the yield to 5.5% for a new buyer ($47.50 divided by $863).

Conversely, you'll be able to increase your bond's price if interest rates decrease and that original 5% return is attractive given a 4.5% return on new bonds. An investor might offer you $1,055 for your bond to lock in a 4.5% return given the $47.50 coupon payment.

Bond prices are quoted in the market on a scale of one hundred. This scale of 100 is what you'll see or what a broker will tell you when buying a bond. A price of 100 means the bond is priced at its face value, usually $1,000 which is also called par value.

If a bond's price is quoted as 85 then it is priced at $850 assuming a $1,000 face value. When a bond is selling for less than 100, less than its face value, then it is said to be selling at a discount.

If a bond's price is quoted as 110 then it is priced at $1,100 and is said to be selling at a premium.

Besides the Fed's decision to raise or lower rates, interest rates can move for a lot of reasons. Most of these have to do with the pace of the economy, other economies around the world and expectations for inflation.

As a long-term investor, you really don't need to worry about interest rates and all the factors that go into bond prices. Economic cycles will come and go, taking bond and stock prices for a ride. Trying to time changes in prices, buying and selling to make a quick profit, is the fastest way to lose money.

Think of your investments more as a savings account with a really great interest rate. Focus more on the money you're putting into the account, put together a simple buy-and-hold strategy like the one outlined at the end of this book and be confident that your money will be there when you need it.

d Yields and Return

$$\frac{\text{coupon payment}}{\text{current price of bond}}$$

$$\frac{\$50}{\$900} = 5.55\% \text{ current yield}$$

The current yield is another measure that you will hear when investing in bonds. It is the coupon payment divided by the current price of the bond. A $900 bond price and a $50 annual coupon mean the bond has a 5.55% current yield.

Don't confuse the coupon rate with the current yield. The coupon rate is set on the face value of the bond and may not be as relevant to new investors. The current yield is the cash return you will get annually if you invest in the bond. After you buy the bond, the current yield may change but will not affect the return you get on your investment.

The **yield to maturity (YTM)** is one of the most important measures and is the return on the bond if you hold it to maturity, including the regular interest payments and the return of the bond's face value when the company buys it back.

The YTM is always provided on bonds because the actual calculation is pretty monstrous. One important consideration is that the calculation assumes that you will be able to reinvest all the interest payments at the same rate. This might not be realistic so the actual return on the bond might be higher or lower depending on how you invest the interest payments.

The **yield to call (YTC)** is another measure of return and appropriate for bonds with a call provision. The call provision means that a company can buy the bond back from investors before the maturity date. If interest rates decrease, a company might want to issue new debt at the lower rate instead of continuing to make payments on older, more expensive bonds.

Lower rates mean your bonds increased in price so you'll probably make money if the company buys them back early. The problem is that now you're stuck with reinvesting the money at lower rates. For this reason, getting called on your bonds is not usually a good thing. Many investors avoid bonds with a call provision even though they may offer a slightly higher return to make up for the possibility of a call happening.

Credit Ratings and Bond Prices

There are three main credit rating agencies; Moody's, Standard & Poor's and Fitch. These rating agencies assess the ability of a company to pay its debt and assign a quality rating to new bond offers. Investors use these ratings to determine whether the bond fits with their own investing strategy and whether the return is enough to justify the risk of investment.

A bond is assigned one of the approximately 20 risk categories. These categories are separated into two groups, investment-grade and non-investment grade. The non-investment grade category is also called speculative or 'junk' bonds.

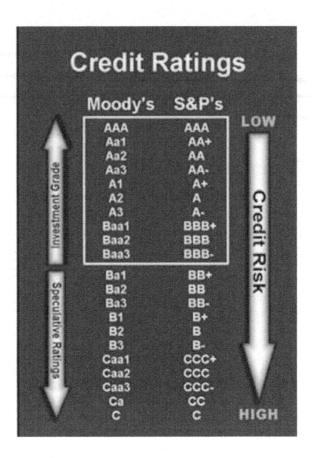

The fact is that there isn't a lot of difference separating the lowest investment grade rating (BBB-) and the highest speculative rating level (BB+). It's an important step though because many companies, like insurance companies and banks, are not allowed to invest in non-investment grade bonds. Bonds in this first non-investment grade risk category often pay very nice returns for a little more risk.

A bond's risk category is used by the issuer to help determine the yield it offers initial investors. Investors will be willing to accept a much lower return on an AAA-rated bond with an almost certain payoff than the return they'll accept to invest in a riskier BB-rated bond.

Rating agencies follow the bonds on which they assign ratings. If a company falls on tough times and it looks more likely that it won't be able to make bond payments, the rating agency might downgrade a bond's credit rating. That means the bond is now in a class of bonds that are paying higher returns to investors because of risk.

Since the payments on the bond do not change, the bond's price must come down to increase the yield. It's the same effect as an increase in interest rates. Conversely, a bond's rating can be upgraded which would send the bond's price higher.

While you may not need to know the details of bond pricing and everything that affects the investment, an understanding of the basics is helpful. Understanding the basic yield measures, credit ratings and other concepts will help you keep a cooler head when pundits start talking about shifting out of bonds ahead of rising interest rates or other risks. While the risk to lower bond prices might be significant for short-term traders, you'll know enough to understand the true long-term potential in your investment and to keep progressing to your goals.

Types of Bonds and the Power of Diversification

Everyone from governments, local authorities, companies and even individuals can offer bonds to investors. You may not need to invest in each type but it's important to know the differences in each type of bond issuer and what it can do for your portfolio.

Bond investing is all about different risks with different issuers. A government can generally raise taxes across a huge population to pay its debt so these bonds are usually safer than others but pay lower yields. Some government or local government bonds may offer tax advantages, offering a special benefit to those in higher tax brackets.

Government Bonds

It may not seem like it around April 15th but the U.S. government regularly needs to raise money by selling bonds. In fact the Unites States owes more than $18 trillion in government debt.

Bonds issued by governments are backed by the "full faith and credit" of the issuer. Bonds issued by the U.S. government are considered a risk-free investment because everyone assumes that Uncle Sam will always pay his bills. Bonds issued by some other countries…not so much.

The risk in government bonds is reflected in their ratings shown in the graphic.

CREDIT RATINGS

LONG-TERM SOVEREIGN DEBT RATINGS

Country/Ratings Agency		Moody's	S&P
U.S.A.		Aaa	AA+
Japan		Aa3	AA−
EURO ZONE			
Austria		Aaa	AAA
Belgium		Aa1	AA+
Cyprus		Baa1	BBB+
Estonia		A1	AA−
Finland		Aaa	AAA
France		Aaa	AAA
Germany		Aaa	AAA
Greece		Ca	CC
Portugal		Ba2	BBB−
Slovakia		A1	A+
Slovenia		Aa3	AA
Spain		A1	AA−

Sources: Moody's, Standard & Poors, Fitch

Of course the difference in risk translates to different returns you'll earn on these government's bonds. The ten-year U.S. Treasury Bond pays just 2.25% annually and Germany's ten-year bond will get you just 0.51% a year.

Invest in riskier governments like Greece and you could earn 7.1% a year...or you could lose everything if the country defaults.

Investment grade government bonds, those rated BBB or better, have defaulted at a rate of less than 1% over more than four decades. Bonds of less financially-stable countries like emerging markets have defaulted at a higher rate but the higher returns can make it worth it.

Historical Default Rate on Government Bonds

Investment Grade	0.62%
Non-Investment Grade	20.05%
All	5.82%

Source: Moody's

Consider two $100,000 portfolios of bonds. One portfolio holds only the bonds of the safest governments and yields 2.25% annually for ten years. At the end of the decade, you'd have $124,900 in the portfolio.

Now consider that the other portfolio invests in riskier government debt at a 5% annual yield but 20% of the portfolio defaults immediately. Even if you received nothing on those defaulted bonds, you would still have $130,300 at the end of ten years. Typically, investors get something back on defaulted government bonds so the return on the riskier portfolio would be even higher. This example may not be realistic because it's unlikely that you'd see all your defaults immediately and collect no interest. It just shows how, even on a much higher default rate, riskier bonds can still yield higher returns.

Besides the potential for higher returns, bonds of foreign countries offer the potential to reduce your overall investing risk as well. As one country is entering recession, meaning more risk on its government's bonds, another country may be experiencing an economic boom.

Foreign bonds are either denominated in dollars or in the local currency. This adds another layer of risk if the local currency rises or falls against the dollar. If your foreign bonds are paid in the local currency, your return will increase if the currency rises against the dollar. Conversely, your return could take a hit if the foreign currency falls against the dollar.

Don't neglect bonds of foreign countries because of the higher default rate. The benefits of diversification through economic cycles and currency can really help reduce risk in your portfolio.

The upside to investing in U.S. Treasury Bonds is that you pay no state or local taxes on the interest payments. You'll still have to pay federal income taxes on the interest, unless held in a retirement account or by a qualified non-profit organization.

Just because government bonds may have very little default risk, don't think they still aren't exposed to other bond risks. Prices for long-term government bonds rise and fall along with interest rates and bonds issued in other currencies will react to changing foreign exchange rates.

There are several different types of government bonds, some with features more like a savings account than a bond investment. We'll look into the options for U.S. bonds though many countries follow the same basic format.

The lowest denomination for U.S. government bonds is the Savings Bond, starting at $25 and for any denomination investment up to $10,000 per year. You can't sell your Savings Bonds to another investor as with other bonds so it's more like a savings account than an investment.

Series EE bonds do not pay interest but sell at a steep discount to their value. The price is half of the face value and interest accrues to the price each year. When you sell the bond, you get the new price including all the accrued interest. You can pay taxes on the accrued interest each year or once when you sell the bonds. You can't sell your bonds within the first year and will give up three months of interest if you sell them in less than five years.

Treasury Inflation-Protected Securities (TIPS) receive an interest payment and an increase in value twice a year to adjust for inflation. TIPS offer protection from the potential for faster inflation but not much else. Rates tend to be extremely low.

There are three types of U.S. Treasury debt:

- Treasury Bills have maturities of a year or less

- Treasury Notes have maturities from two to seven years

- Treasury Bonds have maturities of 10 to 30 years

Despite the different names given these three classes, they are all bonds and the only difference is their maturity date. All are issued electronically and can be bought directly from the Treasury or through a broker. In fact, one big benefit to buying bonds issued by the U.S. government is the ability to buy directly from the government without brokerage fees or a price markup.

Treasury Bills have a face value of $100 each and sell for a discount. When the Bill matures, you receive the full value. Treasury Notes and Bonds sell for their face value and pay a fixed interest rate.

Corporate Bonds

Raising money through debt is an important part of running a business. Issuing bonds means owners can raise money to operate the company without having to share profits with investors. As long as you can make the semi-annual payments and the lump payment at maturity, bonds represent a great source of financial leverage.

Issuing bonds is also a cheaper source of financing for many businesses. A financially stable company can borrow money at 4%

while investors might require double-digit returns to take an ownership position in the business.

The fact that bond payments must be made and represent a debt burden, most companies use a mix of bond and stock financing. Rating agencies can penalize a company with lower ratings if it issues more debt than it can handle. The company will issue as much in low-cost bonds as it can at low rates and then sell shares to cover the rest of its funding needs.

Some companies are so financially-stable that their credit rating is even better than that of the United States government. Over the 35 years to 2006, just half a percent of the bonds issued by the safest companies have defaulted.

Historical Default Rate and Yield on Corporate Bonds

	Default Rate	Ten-year Yield
AAA	0.5%	3.1%
AA	0.9%	3.5%
A	2.2%	4.2%
BBB	5.0%	5.7%
BB	10.9%	7.7%
B	23.6%	7.0%
CCC	47.0%	7.6%

Source: Standard & Poor's (1971 - 2006)

The bonds of riskier companies have a higher chance of defaulting but also offer higher returns. Nearly a quarter of the bonds issued with a B-rating over the same 35 year period defaulted but a portfolio of the bonds still yielded better than 5.5% annually over the period.

Municipal Bonds

Municipal bonds are just like government bonds except issued by local authorities like states, cities and townships. While the bonds might not be backed by the stability of the federal government, most carry a fairly strong rating and carry a great tax advantage.

Besides not owing state or local taxes on the interest payments, you aren't responsible for federal income taxes on the interest either. For investors in higher tax brackets, that's a huge benefit and muni bonds are a popular tax planning strategy.

An investor in the 40% tax bracket investing in U.S. Treasury Bonds earning 2.25% annually might only see a real return of 1.35% after paying federal income taxes. That same investor can invest in an A-rated municipal bond earning 2.7% and keep all the interest without any tax liability.

Investors can compare taxable bonds with tax-free municipal bonds by finding the tax-equivalent yield. This means finding the return you'll need to get on a taxable bond to equal the return available on a tax-free municipal bond. To do this, you simply divide the yield on the muni bond by one minus your tax rate (1-tax rate).

If a municipal bond offers a yield of 2.7% annually and you're in the 25% tax bracket then you divide 2.7% by 0.75 to get 3.6 percent. Any taxable corporate or Treasury bond would need to offer a yield of 3.6% to offer the same after-tax return as the comparable municipal bond.

Of course, comparing bonds by yield means comparing bonds of the same rating category and with similar maturity dates.

Muni bonds are generally one of two types, general obligation (GO) bonds or revenue bonds.

GO bonds usually have a lower default rate compared to revenue bonds because the payment for the bonds is backed by a broader revenue stream, the local tax base. Revenue bonds are only backed by the cash generated from a specific project. If the cash flows on the project, say a toll-road expansion, are not enough to make payments then the bond might default.

Municipal defaults have been a hot topic over the past several years with the default of Detroit and the potential for a default on Puerto Rico bonds. Municipal bonds have always been seen as extremely safe investments and some are even backed with insurance against a default. Pension funds and insurance companies are heavily invested in municipal bonds for their safety and the potential for default has caught a lot of investors off-guard.

Despite the media hype over defaults or the potential for defaults of some large municipal bond offers, most muni bonds are still extremely safe. According to data from Moody's, there has never been a default of an AAA-rated muni bond. Just 0.04% of A-rated bonds defaulted over the four decades to 2011, that's just one default in every 2,500 bond issues at that rating category.

Overall, only 0.13% of all muni bonds defaulted over the 41-year period and investors have earned a 2.73% annual return on a tax-adjusted basis.

Peer Lending as a Bond Investment

Peer lending is emerging as an interesting part of investors' bond options. Peer lending sites like Prosper and Lending Club connect investors directly with unsecured loans to small businesses and individuals.

These loans are legal contracts and go on the borrower's credit report but are not rated by credit agencies. The peer lending site issues a rating based on the borrower's credit history and the loan.

Peer loans have a fixed payment that is deposited in your account on a monthly basis and a fixed maturity, usually either three or five years. Unlike traditional bonds, peer loan payments include interest and the principal. The monthly payment you receive will be higher but you won't receive a large lump-sum payment when the loan matures.

Since peer loans are not backed by company assets or the tax base of a government, risk is considerably higher on the investment. Default rates are higher for peer loans but the return is also higher.

Risk and Return on Peer Loans

	Default Rate	Average Annual Return
A	2.2%	5.2%
B	4.8%	7.3%
C	7.4%	8.7%
D	10.7%	8.9%
E	14.3%	9.5%
F/G	18.6%	8.8%
All	7.6%	8.0%

Source: Lending Club, November 2015
Loans issued from 2007 through 2014

The process of investing in peer loans is straight-forward and fees are generally lower than investing in other bonds. Fees on loans are paid by borrowers though investors may have to pay annual account fees.

Because of the higher defaults on peer loans, the investment should be a part of the high-yield (junk) portion of your bond portfolio. We'll go further into how much money of your total portfolio to allocate to each type of bond later in the book.

How the Bond Market Works

Bonds are bought through a broker, much like it's done when you buy stocks. Unlike stocks though, where you usually pay a commission, most brokers make their money through a markup on the price.

After deciding on the bond you want to buy or an idea of the maturity and rating you want, your broker can help by quoting a few bonds available. The broker is going to quote the price at which they are willing to sell you the bond which will be higher than the price they pay to buy it from another investor.

This system used to be heavily stacked against regular investors because you never really knew how much your broker was making when you bought or sold a bond.

Thanks to a new electronic reporting system called TRACE, managed by the Financial Industry Regulatory Authority (FINRA), you can see the prices paid for bonds to see exactly how much your broker is making. Bonds are quoted on two prices, the bid price and the ask price. The bid price is the price at which someone is offering to sell the bond. The ask is the price at which someone is offering to buy the bond.

Through the TRACE system, you can see how much investors are paying for a specific bond or how much of a markup your broker typically asks for in a trade. Before agreeing to buy a bond through a broker, it's a good idea to check out the current prices. This will tell you how much the broker is marking up your price and you might be able to negotiate a lower price.

Buying your bonds through a large money manager like Vanguard or through an online trading platform like Schwab or E*Trade is usually the lowest-cost option. The large brokerage firms may be able to sell bonds with a smaller markup because they buy and sell so frequently that they still make billions. Online trading platforms often charge a small fee per bond traded but then offer smaller markups on the price.

If you are not buying your bonds through one of the larger companies like Fidelity or Vanguard, or through an online trading site, make sure you check out the TRACE system to see how much your broker is marking up prices.

Not only is selling your bonds before they mature generally a bad idea but costs tend to be higher as well. There may be fewer investors that want a bond if it is maturing within a few years and you may have to take a pretty big cut in price. Broker markups for buying bonds are not generally as high as when you go to sell.

Why I don't like bond funds...but why you will love them

Besides investing in individual bonds, you can also invest in funds that hold a variety of bonds. Like stocks, this is done through mutual funds or exchange traded funds (ETFs). These funds are professionally managed according to fund rules to buy and sell individual bonds.

You can buy bond funds just as easily as buying a share of stock. ETFs trade just like stocks and most carry a management fee of less than 0.5% annually.

Bond funds carry a lot of advantages, especially for investors with less than a few hundred thousand dollars. Buying into a bond fund gives you instant diversification across hundreds or even thousands of bond issuers. It's difficult for regular investors to buy enough bonds to get that kind of diversification across rating and maturity.

Bond funds also allow for easy and cost-effective reinvestment of interest. On a four percent coupon, you'll receive $400 annually for every $10,000 of bonds you own. The fees and markup on buying just a few bonds at a time can really add up so you might not be able to reinvest your interest in new bonds until old bonds mature. This could mean several years of interest just sitting in your account without earning a return.

Reinvesting your interest payments regularly in bond funds gets the money working for you quickly and at a lower cost than buying smaller amounts of individual bonds. We'll cover a reinvestment strategy to take advantage of funds in the step-by-step portion of the book.

Despite the advantage of bond funds, there are several disadvantages as well.

Bond funds may not offer the same maturity benefits compared to individual bonds. While each individual bond held by the fund has a maturity date, the fund itself will never mature. This means investors do not benefit from the certainty of a yield to maturity. The fund manager will be constantly buying and selling bonds.

Some bonds may mature but the lack of a yield to maturity means investors may not be able to plan their return as definitively as with individual bonds. Don't be misled when the bond fund reports an 'average' yield to maturity. That's just the average YTM of the bonds held but means little for investors in the fund.

Funds also do not offer a fixed payment on the investment. Each bond held by the fund will have a fixed payment but the overall fund payment will change depending on the actions of the fund manager. Funds usually pay dividends quarterly from the interest payments but these dividend payments will change depending on the change in bonds held by the fund.

For many investors, bond investing is about these certainties in yield and semi-annual payments. Against the extreme volatility of the stock market, the relative certainty of return in bonds is the biggest reason to invest in individual bonds. Investors depending on consistent bond payments to cover living expenses may find it harder to plan their investments with bond funds and the less consistent payment stream from the fund.

Still, the benefits to investing in bond funds outweigh the disadvantages and some investors may prefer funds over individual bonds. It will be difficult for anyone with less than $100,000 to invest in bonds to get the diversification needed in individual bonds and will really eat into returns.

To really diversify your bond portfolio and minimize the effects of interest rates, defaults and other risks, an individual bond portfolio needs a mix of bonds across maturities, issuer types and rating categories. Investing in government bonds, corporates and municipal bonds in three rating categories each and three maturities means you'd need to invest across 27 bonds. Buying just a few thousand of each bond will mean broker markups will seriously eat into your return but buying $5k or more of each means the broker markup may not be as high a percentage of each investment.

The best strategy is one that uses a mix of both individual bonds and bond funds, taking advantage of lower costs in funds to reinvest interest payments while using individual bonds to reinvest the base amount. We'll cover different strategies to use bond funds and individual bonds depending on your total portfolio size in the next section.

A Step-by-Step Bond Investing Strategy

Bond investing can be as complicated as you make it. Careers have been made on bond analysis, buying and selling the investments at the right time to make a few percentage points more.

The jury is out as to whether this kind of investing is even worth it or can provide investors with a return over simpler strategies. Several studies have shown that most fund managers don't beat a simple buy-and-hold strategy after accounting for fees.

The fact is that you really don't need a complicated investing strategy or a money manager to meet your financial goals. I've been an investment analyst for nearly a decade and can tell you that, most often, the only people that make money on complicated trading strategies are those collecting the trading fees.

Putting together a simple investing strategy according to your own needs will do two important things for you. First, it puts you directly in control of your own financial future. You won't have to worry about some money manager making self-interested decisions to increase their own fees or stealing your money outright.

Putting together a simple strategy can also take the stress out of reaching your goals. A money manager is tasked with constantly reaching for higher returns and 'beating' the market to justify their added expense. That means taking risks on your money and the potential to miss your goals. Planning your own portfolio around a simple and safe strategy means you can be confident that you will reach your financial goals ahead of retirement.

That simple concept is what the step-by-step investing series is all about. Each of the books in the series shows you how to put together a simple buy-and-hold strategy according to your needs and how to maintain that strategy over decades of investment.

Step 1: How much do you need in bonds?

Starting your bond investing strategy means understanding the annual investment return you need each year to retirement and the level of risk you're comfortable taking.

We've covered how to plan out your retirement goals, annual return needed and your risk tolerance in the other three books in the step-by-step series. It's a fairly straight-forward process and you don't need an exact number but it's critical that you start with your own needs.

- Start with the amount of money you'll need in retirement. Adjust your current expenses by any plans for travel or other things you want to do. You'll spend more on healthcare and less in other areas but the general rule is about 80% of your current expenses.

- Multiply the amount you'll need in retirement on an annual basis by 25 times. This is based on the idea that you can safely withdraw 4% (one-twenty fifth) of your portfolio each year in retirement without worrying about running out of money. You might be able to get away with 20-times the amount you need, withdrawing 5% a year, but its best to start planning with conservative numbers.

- Use an online retirement calculator to find your annual return needed on investments given your current investments, target amount and how much you are able to save each month.

- Understand your level of risk tolerance through your ability and willingness for risk. Your risk tolerance is like a check against your need for return.

- If you need a high rate of return, upwards of 8% annually, you'll need to invest a greater amount to stocks but only if you have a high tolerance for risk. If your tolerance for risk does not match your need for return, then you are likely to miss your goals through bad investor behaviors like panic-selling.

- Conversely, if you have a higher tolerance for risk but a low rate of return needed, you might be able to reevaluate your retirement goals and seek a little higher return.

Investing without knowing your need for return and tolerance for risk is like heading out for a road trip without a destination. You will end up trading in and out of investments, paying way too much in fees and never realize the benefits of a well-organized plan to reach your financial destination.

One of the biggest reasons investors neglect bonds is because they don't really know what kind of return they need to reach their financial goals. They assume that investing is about reaching for the highest possible return and look to other investments where risk is higher. Investors end up almost exclusively in stocks, get caught in the market's rollercoaster mania and panic-sell their way to the poor house.

Actually planning out their investments and the annual return needed to reach retirement goals, most investors are surprised by just how little risk they need to take. I reevaluated my own goals several years ago and found that I needed an annual return of less than 5% to grow my portfolio large enough to pay for retirement expenses. With a new return target, I was able to increase my investment in bonds and reduce overall risk.

From the level of return you need annually to reach your goals and your comfort level with risk, you can start putting your investing strategy together with an asset allocation plan.

Asset allocation is just a way of saying how you will invest your total wealth across the asset classes like stocks, bonds and real estate. Each asset class carries different levels of risk as well as different types of risk. Inflation is one of the biggest risks in bonds, reducing the purchasing power of your semi-annual coupons, while real estate prices tend to rise at least at the pace of annual inflation.

Investing at least a little in stocks, bonds and real estate will help reduce your overall risk to any particular factor and smooth your annual returns.

Bonds as a group returned 4.6% annually over the decade to 2013. While there's no guarantee that bonds will offer the same return going forward, we can use past returns as a benchmark for asset allocation.

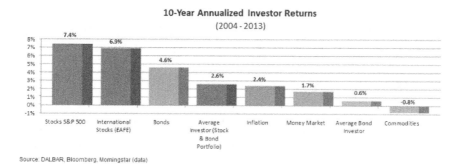

10-Year Annualized Investor Returns
(2004 - 2013)

Source: DALBAR, Bloomberg, Morningstar (data)

The actual long-term return on your bond portfolio may change over time and will be more complicated than simply looking at the average yield-to-maturity on the individual bonds. What you do with the semi-annual interest payments will have a lot to do with your actual returns. If you are able to reinvest your interest payments at higher rates, as interest rates increase, then the long-term return on your bond portfolio will gradually increase. If you do not reinvest your interest payments frequently or are forced to invest in lower yield bonds as rates fall, then your long-term return may be lower than initially planned.

There are a few other hurdles to figuring out your actual return on a bond but they're not quite as important if you plan on holding your bonds to maturity.

- You can book a higher return by selling your bonds when rates decrease and prices rise, but then you're stuck buying new bonds at lower rates.

- Inflation might eat into bond prices, changing your return if you sell after bonds have dropped. We'll look at a laddering strategy later that will minimize the effect of inflation on your bond portfolio.

Trying to emphasize the importance of building a portfolio around your own risk tolerance and return needs, I hesitate to suggest a percentage you should have in bonds at different stages in your life. I've used the following graphic as an example in other books and it seems to show the changing nature of asset allocation rather well.

Life Stage Investing - Matching Risk with Your Needs

Stocks	70%	60%	50%	30%
Bonds	15%	15%	25%	50%
Real Estate	15%	25%	25%	20%

* Percentages are approximate and may not be appropriate for all investors

Starting out in your 20s or 30s, you'll have a great deal of time before retirement and can take a little more investing risk. Use this ability to tolerate risk to get higher returns on your investments through more money in stocks. Most younger investors will hold the majority of their portfolio in stocks.

Don't neglect bonds and real estate completely as a younger investor. Getting started investing in bonds early will help avoid putting it off like so many investors do. Not only do bonds provide stability but they can also help protect your money while you wait for lower stock prices in which to invest.

As you get older and closer to retirement, your risk tolerance will decrease. You'll want to revisit your allocation to the three assets every ten years to reduce the risk in your portfolio. Leaving your investments mostly in stocks until you're ready to retire will leave you exposed to a stock market crash at exactly the wrong time.

For those that want a little less risk, you might try increasing the percentage of your portfolio in bonds though I don't think it should ever be more than 80% of your total wealth. Putting all your money in bonds leaves you too exposed to faster inflation and returns that might not be high enough to meet your goals.

Holding 50% to 70% of your total wealth in bonds during retirement is probably enough for most people. You'll benefit from the higher growth in stocks and protection against inflation but you'll have enough in bonds that you won't have to worry about stock prices. In the event of a crash in stock prices, you will be able to withdraw from your bond portfolio until stock prices rebound.

Besides changing your allocation across assets according to your changing risk tolerance, you can also change your investments within the asset classes. A portfolio with a high allocation to stocks may still be relatively safe if it's in safer companies like utilities and consumer staples. Conversely, a portfolio mostly in bonds could be extremely risky if it's all in junk bonds or risky peer loans.

I talk more about reducing your risk within the specific asset classes by diversifying across sectors in the first book in the series, Step-by-Step Investing.

Step 2: Which bonds are right for you?

After deciding how much of your money to put into bonds, you'll need to decide how much to invest in the different bond types as well as different maturities and ratings.

As with the asset classes and other investments, the idea here is to diversify your bond portfolio within bonds to smooth returns and best fit your needs.

Even if you have several decades to retirement, you'll want to buy some shorter-term bonds so you can reinvest money if interest rates increase. Longer-term bonds will offer higher current rates but will lock you into those rates for the period.

Since interest payments are taxed as income, you'll need to watch how much you make in interest payments each year. If interest payments mean a higher tax rate then you might want to put more money in tax-free municipal bonds or adjust the amount in tax-deferred retirement accounts.

While riskier bonds offer a higher yield, an economic recession might increase default rates and lower the yield you get on the portfolio. Include a mix of safer bonds along with lower-rated bonds according to your risk tolerance.

In fact, while safe investment-grade bonds are relatively uncorrelated with the stock market, junk bonds tend to follow the market more closely. With investment-grade bonds, it's highly likely that the issuer will be able to repay the loan. This makes things like interest rate changes and inflation the biggest factors in prices.

For non-investment grade bonds, the company's or country's ability to repay the debt is the big question mark. In a recession, the ability to repay may be even more in doubt and the bond's price could fall considerably with a rating downgrade. Actual defaults will also pick up during an economic recession. During a recession, the value of your junk bonds will likely decrease though not nearly as much as the value of stocks.

I've included a chart of current rates on 10-year bonds for municipals and corporate debt at different ratings. Average rates on government bonds are difficult to find because yields vary according to relative inflation and interest rates in each country. Don't forget to consider U.S. and other government bonds for your diversified portfolio.

Average Yields on 10-year Bonds
(November 2015)

	Muni	Corporate
AAA	2.26%	3.03%
A	3.37%	4.25%
BBB	4.25%	5.71%
High Yield	4.60%	8.06%

Source: Bloomberg

Deciding in which investment accounts to hold your bonds can mean a big difference in returns. You will want to hold your municipal bonds in taxable accounts since the investment is already tax-advantaged. You may be responsible for paying taxes to a foreign government on your foreign bonds but will generally receive a credit on your U.S. taxes so these should also be held in taxable investing accounts to take advantage of that tax credit.

Other taxable bonds like corporate bonds and peer loans should be held in tax-advantaged retirement accounts. This will protect you from the income tax bite on interest payments.

U.S. Treasury bonds can be held in either a taxed or a tax-advantaged account. Holding them in your retirement account will protect interest payments from federal income taxes but you might not be able to hold all your investments in these accounts. If you've already maxed out your retirement contributions on other investments, holding treasuries in a taxable account still offers the advantage of saving on state and local taxes.

While peer lending is yet to be a widely accepted class for bond investors, I don't think it will be long before it gains widespread approval. It's true that peer loans involve more risk than conventional bonds but they also offer a great bridge between the higher returns of stocks and the certainty of bonds.

Because of the higher risk involved with high-yield (junk) bonds and in peer loans, I would allocate no more than 30% of your bond portfolio to both groups. Note that isn't 30% of your total wealth but 30% of your bond portfolio. If you hold 50% of your total wealth in bonds then it would mean less than 15% (30% of 50%) in higher risk bond investments. This gives your bond portfolio a chance at slightly higher returns but still the relative safety from higher-rated bonds.

Check out the average rates on different maturities across government, municipals and corporate bonds on Bloomberg or one of the other resources available at the end of the book. This will help you plan out how much to allocate to each bond type and maturity to arrive at the return you need.

You will want to put together something like the example table below with available rates in each bond type and by different time periods. Peer loans are only available for three- and five-year loans and high-yield bonds are generally only issued at 10-year or less maturities.

Buying bonds across short-term, intermediate and long-term time horizons will stagger your investment by time. This will help to balance interest rate and reinvestment risk because you'll be able to reinvest your shorter-term bonds fairly soon while still benefiting from higher current rates on your long-term bonds.

Don't think you need to allocate an equal amount of money to each issuer and each time period. With a little more risk tolerance, you might allocate more to corporate bonds, high yield and peer loans.

	Government	Muni	Corporate	Peer Loan
5-year AAA	1.64%	1.05%	1.65%	5.00%
5-year BBB		3.40%	4.50%	8.00%
5-year High Yield		4.10%	5.40%	9.00%
10-year AAA	2.25%	2.03%	3.03%	NA
10-year BBB	5.25%	4.05%	5.71%	NA
10-year High Yield	5.71%	4.60%	8.06%	NA
20-year AAA	2.50%	2.81%	3.73%	NA
20-year BBB		7.03%	7.11%	NA

* Rates only an example - check actual rates before you invest

As an example:

A relatively low-risk portfolio might hold 60% in government and municipal bonds, 30% in corporate bonds and 10% in high-yield and peer loans. This allocation benefits from tax advantages and stability in government bonds while still providing higher returns from corporate and higher-risk bonds. Investing fairly equal amounts across short-term, intermediate and long-term bonds makes the strategy a little simpler and helps spread your investments out further. Don't forget to include foreign government and corporate bonds for added diversification and return.

A higher-risk portfolio might hold 20% in government/municipal bonds, 60% in corporate bonds and 30% in high-yield and peer loans. This allocation will still provide some safety in government bonds while increasing the overall return through corporate and higher-risk bonds.

There's no "perfect" allocation for any investor and don't worry too much about picking exact percentages in each bond type. The idea is to target a rough proportion within each bond class to help see what kind of return you can expect. While corporate and high-yield bonds may involve more risk compared to government bonds, most are still lower risk than stocks.

To estimate the return on your total portfolio of bonds, you multiply the percentage of the portfolio by the average return in each group of bonds. If you have 20% of your portfolio in government bonds and the average yield to maturity of your government bonds is 3% then that part of your bond portfolio will provide about 0.6% return (20% times 3%) to your total portfolio. Put together a table like the one below to estimate your total bond portfolio return on different allocations to bond types. It may seem like a lot of math but it's pretty simple with a spreadsheet. Remember to adjust municipal bond yields for taxes to make the return comparable with other bonds.

Estimating Your Bond Portfolio Return

	Percentage of Your Bond Portfolio	Average Return	Contribution to Portfolio Return
Government Bonds	20.0%	3.0%	0.60%
Corporates	40.0%	4.5%	1.80%
Municipals	20.0%	4.0%	0.80%
High Yield	10.0%	5.5%	0.55%
Peer Loans	10.0%	6.0%	0.60%
Estimated Return on Bonds			4.35%

* Municipal bond returns should be tax-adjusted

This is the same way you would estimate the total return to entire portfolio across bonds, stocks and real estate. You take the estimated return in each asset class and multiply it by the percentage of your total wealth in the asset class. Adding up each of the three will give you an estimate of your annual return on your wealth which you can compare against the annual return you need to meet your financial goals.

Step 3: How to choose and buy bonds for your portfolio

Picking individual bonds can actually be fairly easy because the credit rating agencies do the analysis legwork for you. The credit rating agencies rate bonds across four primary measures called the four C's of credit.

- Character is the history of the company, management's experience and any history of bond payments.

- Capacity is the financial ability of the company to make the bond payments. It includes the current amount of debt and payments as well as if the company has more credit available from banks or other companies.

- Capital is the assets and other resources owned by the company that can be used to repay debt or generate sales.

- Condition includes external factors that might affect the company's ability to repay debt like industry growth, currency fluctuations and the economy.

You could spend hours and even days studying individual bond offers and companies, comparing the bond against others in the same rating category, but it generally won't make much difference in your returns. It's a lot like trying to pick individual stocks and hoping to "beat" the rest of the market by finding something nobody else sees. Bonds within each rating category tend to be fairly similar as far as risk and return so don't spend your time worrying about which individual bonds to choose within each rating category. Focus more on choosing a mix of bonds across risk categories, issuer types and maturities.

Some investors have brought up the problem of conflict in bond ratings over recent years, especially following the financial crisis of 2008. While rating agencies are supposed to assign ratings impartially and according to an objective process, there is a conflict in the system.

Companies pay rating agencies to assign a rating on the bonds they issue. A rating agency that constantly assigns lower ratings to bond offers compared to other agencies may find its rating subscribers go to other agencies for more favorable ratings. There's some evidence to support the argument but historical default rates do not seem to suggest that the conflict is significant. If the conflict of interest was too significant then you would expect much higher defaults on even safer investment-grade bonds.

Call provisions within a bond will generally mean higher yields offered but the bonds could be called before maturity if interest rates fall. This could mean that your return on bonds is lower than you expected because you'll have to reinvest the money at lower rates instead of benefiting from the return on the original bond. It could also mean that you'll need to pay another markup spread to a broker to reinvest your money into a new bond.

Check your potential picks for call provision and the difference in interest rates before you buy. On callable bonds, you'll want to compare the yield-to-call rate because that is the return you'll get if the bond is called. If the YTM is higher than the YTC then the bond is likely to get called early by the company. The simplest strategy is just to avoid callable bonds all-together.

Laddering your Bond Portfolio

Buying bonds of different maturities isn't only a good idea to balance interest rate and reinvestment risk but it's also a great way to plan the flow of cash from your investments.

The technique is called laddering and involves buying bonds that mature at different dates to coincide with your cash flow needs and expenses. While your semi-annual interest payments might cover a good portion of your living expenses in retirement, they might not cover everything. Laddering your bonds means you can use the maturing bonds to cover additional expenses instead of having to sell bonds.

The idea is pretty simple and works while you are reinvesting your bonds as well as when you start using proceeds for expenses.

When buying bonds for your portfolio, spread your investment across many different maturity years.

If you're planning on reinvesting the money when bonds mature, spread your maturities out every few years. Buy bonds that mature within equal intervals from five years to 20 or 30 years. Every five years, when some bonds mature, reinvest the proceeds in a new group of bonds that mature five years from the longest-maturity bonds.

Climbing the Bond Ladder

In a laddered bond strategy, maturing short-term bonds are reinvested in bonds at the ladder's long end, which typically offers higher yields. The strategy can provide constant income or protect from interest-rate changes.

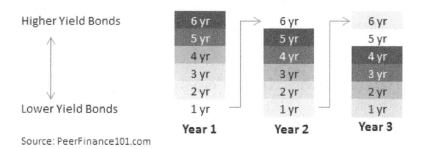

Source: PeerFinance101.com

If you are planning on using maturing bonds to help pay for living expenses, you will want to buy bonds that mature every year or two. This will mean a more frequent stream of bonds maturing for a consistent cash flow.

Using Bond Funds with Your Portfolio

While I haven't talked much about bond funds, it's important to include them in your bond investing strategy. In fact, if your total bond portfolio is less than $100k, you may want to stay in bond funds entirely. With less than this amount to invest in individual bonds, the investments across bond type, maturity and rating will be so small that you will end up paying a large percentage of your portfolio in broker markup and fees.

If you are investing exclusively in bond funds, choose a mix of bond funds that give you exposure to different issuer types, maturities and risk levels. It's pretty easy to build a diversified mix of bond funds and really cost-effective. Buy these funds through your online stock investing platform just as you would a share of stock.

Some good bond ETFs to consider for your portfolio:

iShares 20+ Year Treasury Bond (TLT) holds long-term U.S. government bonds with maturities of twenty years and longer.

iShares Core U.S. Aggregate Bond (AGG) attempts to track the performance of the U.S. bond market. It holds investment-grade corporate bonds, Treasuries, mortgage-backed bonds and other fixed bonds.

iShares Investment Grade Corporate Bond (LQD) provides exposure to the broad U.S. investment-grade corporate bond market. Bond maturities are spread out from three years through 20+ years.

Vanguard Total International Bond ETF (BNDX) invests in bonds issued outside the United States including governments and corporations. Most of the bonds are from Europe (57%) or Asia/Pacific (28%) with varying credit qualities and maturities.

SPDR Barclays High Yield Bond ETF (JNK) invests in non-investment grade corporate bonds. Most of the bonds are rated B or BB with a small percentage rated CCC or lower. Since most investment grade bonds are issued at shorter maturities, most of the bonds in the fund mature between three to ten years.

If you plan on investing more than $100,000 in bonds, you might look to individual bonds for investment. On this strategy, I would invest the entire amount in individual bonds and then use bond funds to reinvest the interest payments every six months. Waiting six months to reinvest interest payments helps to reduce commissions paid on bond funds. When individual bonds mature, the money can be reinvested in other bonds to maintain your overall exposure.

Don't forget that you can buy U.S. Treasury bonds with no markup or fee on the TreasuryDirect website. Along with the tax advantage on state and local taxes, this can help to make the yield on government bonds much more persuasive against those on other bonds.

Step 4: Maintaining your bond portfolio

The best way to maintain your bond portfolio is to not worry about your bond portfolio. Bonds serve their purpose best when held to maturity, minimizing trading fees and making returns more certain.

Don't listen to bond brokers, even one with a good track record for analysis and market timing. Brokers only make money when you buy or sell. They'll find reasons to call and why you should sell but don't do it.

If you are holding your taxable bonds in retirement accounts, you won't have to worry much about taxes on interest payments. If you do hold some bonds in a taxable investment account, don't forget to plan for taxes. If you are going to owe higher income taxes due to bond interest, make sure you keep some money available so you don't have to sell investments come tax time.

If you sell your bonds, you may also be on the hook for capital gains taxes if you sell for a price higher than the purchase price. While it may seem like a no-brainer to book a higher return by selling your bonds when prices are right, don't forget to deduct this amount for taxes when you compare returns. If you plan on keeping the same total amount in bonds, you'll also need to pay a fee and markup on a new bond.

After accounting for the tax bite, money paid to a broker on a new bond and the possibility of reinvesting at lower rates – you're almost always better off just holding your bonds until they mature.

Remember the 'normal' yield curve and the idea that longer-term bonds pay higher interest rates? From time to time, this idea gets turned on its head and results in what's called an inverted yield curve. When this happens, long-term bonds pay lower rates than bonds maturing over the next few years.

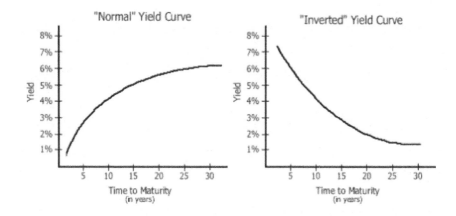

Why does this happen and should it affect how you invest in your bond portfolio?

Understand that a big part of the yield curve is the market's (investor's) perception of where interest rates will be in the future. If investors believe that interest rates will be lower, usually because of economic problems or lower inflation, then they may accept lower rates on bonds over that period in the future.

Many investors see an inverted yield curve and stop investing in longer-term bonds. After all, why invest in a 30-year bond when you can get a better rate by investing in shorter-term bonds? Worse yet, many investors see lower rates in bonds and shift their money to stocks trying to squeak out a little higher yield.

The reason you shouldn't let the shape of the yield curve affect how you invest or reinvest your bond money is because of what usually follows an inverted yield curve.

The yield curve has inverted before every recession for the last 50 years. That's a perfect seven-for-seven call on the next recession. The stock market often peaks right around the time the yield curve inverts and recession hits within about five to 16 months afterwards.

If the economy does fall into a recession, you'll want those longer-term bonds to protect your portfolio. When interest rates come down as the Fed deals with lower growth, the prices on long-term bonds will increase at a faster pace.

Resist the temptation to change your investing strategy when the yield curve inverts. Try to reinvest your money along the same target percentages you previously set.

When to sell your bonds

The best answer as to when to sell your bonds is never. Selling your bonds will mean extra broker fees and possibly capital gains taxes. You are not likely to consistently find cheaper bonds so there is little point to trading in and out of your bond investments.

There are really only two scenarios that I would consider selling my bonds before maturity.

- If the stock market has fallen 25% or more and I need to rebalance my overall portfolio on the change in values. If you have 50% of your total wealth in stocks and the stock market falls by 25%, you would now have just 37.5% of your wealth in stocks (assuming other asset classes didn't change). You might then want to move some money from bonds to stocks to get your percentages back on target.

- Older investors depending on their investments for living expenses may find that regular interest payments don't cover all their needs. This problem can be minimized by laddering your bonds, using regular bond maturities to help pay for expenses, but you may still need to sell bonds from time to time.

A Special Request

I hope you've enjoyed Step-by-Step Bond Investing and found the advice to be helpful in putting together your bond strategy. Throughout the book, I've tried to emphasize the benefit to a simple and basic strategy that meets YOUR financial goals. There's no lack of ways to complicate your investing strategy but the simplest approach will get you to where you want to be with the least amount of headache and sleepless nights.

I'd like to ask one favor as you finish reading the book. Reader reviews are extremely important to the success of a book on Amazon. Reviews play a big part in determining the rank of a book and how many people see it when searching.

If you found the book to be helpful, would you please leave a review on the Amazon page?

It's really easy to do and does not have to be a long, detailed review.

Please click here to leave a review on Amazon

- Just go to the book's page on Amazon (or through the link above) and click on "customer reviews" or scroll down and click on "Write a customer review"

- Your review can be as short as a sentence or as long as you like. Just try describing what you liked about the book and any particular points from a chapter.

I always appreciate honest reviews. Thank you so much!

Resources

Round out your investing plan with the best investments in dividends, emerging markets and bonds. Check out the other three books in the Step-by-Step series:

Learn the secret to building an investing strategy that will meet YOUR needs. The first book in the series covers 10 basic rules of investing you must remember to avoid losing money. You'll get the secret to winning the stock market game as well as a step-by-step strategy for buying stocks. *Click here to buy Step-by-Step Investing.*

Learn how to put dividend stocks in your portfolio and money in your pocket! This book covers income investments like REITs, MLPs and dividend stocks that have provided strong returns and a regular cash return. *Click here to buy Step-by-Step Dividend Investing.*

Learn how to add growth to your investments through stocks from the fastest growing countries in the world. This book shows you how to boost returns and lower risk by diversifying in emerging markets. *Click here to buy Step-by-Step Emerging Market Investing.*

See through the BS and scams in passive income strategies to start building a real source of income today in blogging, real estate, stocks and bonds.

NO fluff, NO theories, and NO sugar coating – just the detailed process on how I put together an income from four sources and make money whether I work or not. *Click here to buy The Passive Income Myth*.

News and Professional Organizations

Check out these websites for news and detailed data on investments covered in this book.

Bloomberg – Business and finance news resource that keeps it objective. You'll see some analyst commentary but the ideas are usually fairly balanced.

Morningstar – Professional source of data and company financial information. There is a lot of analysis and advice on the site. Most of it is objective and helpful but avoid using it to make short-term investment decisions.

FINRA Corporate Bond Data – the TRACE system shows bond market transactions as well as a daily recap of market activity. Use it to make sure your broker is not taking a huge cut of your bonds

TreasuryDirect – lets you buy U.S. Treasury bonds including TIPS, EE and I bonds directly from the Treasury. There's no markup or fees so it's a very cost-effective way to buy.

FINRA BrokerCheck – provides information on registered brokers including work history, criminal convictions and client complaints.

Yahoo Finance – An excellent resource for stock information including charts, data and headlines.

Investing and Personal Finance Blogs

Check out these blogs for more advice on personal finance and meeting your long-term goals. Blogs here were chosen for their rational and measured perspective, favoring a long-term approach instead of get-rich-quick schemes.

PeerFinance101 – My blog on personal finance and achieving financial freedom. Financial freedom isn't about getting rich but getting the life you want and making money decisions around that goal. Share your own stories of financial success or learn from others stories.

Side Hustle Nation–A community of part-time entrepreneurs earning financial independence through small business. It's a great resource for finding your passion and turning your hobby into a money-maker.

Barbara Friedberg Personal Finance–Barbara worked as an investment portfolio manager before launching her blog, offering advice following many of the tenets in this book. It's a great site focused on investing and building wealth.

Club Thrifty – Holly and Greg were able to ditch their 9-to-5 jobs after learning to manage their money. The blog focuses on ways to spend smartly, cut debt and earn extra income.

Bible Money Matters – Peter hits all the topics in personal finance but he also talks about faith and family. It's a great blog that will help you lead an inspired life.

Made in United States
Orlando, FL
24 January 2023

29007269R00036